VOLLEYBALL

(FRONTISPIECE) *Henry Bergmann, top-rated beach volleyball player, spikes past the block of Bob Vogelsang. Bergmann, who has also played in international volleyball competition indoors, is pictured throughout this book demonstrating the basic volleyball skills and techniques.* (PHOTO: KEN GATHERUM)

VOLLEYBALL

Dewey Schurman

NEW YORK   1974   **ATHENEUM**

253387

Acknowledgments

THIS BOOK would not have been the same without the help of the players. With particular thanks, I'd like to mention the help given to me by Henry Bergmann, Bob Moore, Bob Van Wagner, Rudy Suwara, Mike Wilton, and Ron Lang.

The photography is by Jim Rush.

Contents

VOLLEYBALL

Introduction

IT'S NO COINCIDENCE that indoor volleyball in the United States has long been dominated by teams from southern California.

Many of the top indoor players on the West Coast learned the game on local beaches, and coaches point to the year-round good weather, the conditioning that comes from playing in the sand, and the level of beach competition as some of the reasons behind the success of the Californians.

At the same time, it's ironic that on the international volleyball scene the strongest teams in recent years have come from Japan, Russia, and East Germany rather than the United States, where volleyball was invented in 1895 at a Massachusetts YMCA.

Played by an estimated 60 million people worldwide,

3

volleyball is much more highly regarded as a sport in several other countries than in the United States, where it's still sometimes seen as a game played over droopy nets during playground picnics and school gym classes.

There are some signs that volleyball in this country is finally beginning to shake that image and be recognized for what it is — a fast, high-powered sport where top athletes can spike balls at speeds of a hundred miles an hour:

● The Big Dippers, an all-star volleyball team led by basketball great Wilt Chamberlain, has toured the nation to sellout crowds in Chicago, Los Angeles, Portland, and New York.

● Mike O'Hara, former U.S. Olympic volleyball standout and founder of the newest professional sports venture, the International Track Association, predicts that volleyball will be the next major professional sport.

● Last year's National Collegiate Athletic Association volleyball championships between host San Diego State and Cal State Long Beach drew 8,412 spectators. In baseball the same night, the Phillies played the Padres in San Diego before a hometown crowd of only 7,261.

● A high school volleyball league formed two years ago in southern California has grown from six to forty-five schools, headed by Palisades High, winner of four straight national American Athletic Union prep division championships.

4

A good part of this book deals with sand-court volleyball and the way it is played on California beaches.

Of course, a volleyball court can be set up almost anywhere — on cement, asphalt, or grass, as well as indoors or on sand. But most players feel that the game is easiest and most fun to learn on the sand, where you can dive for the ball or fall down without fear of injury.

Volleyball players who learn and develop their game on sand are almost always good *all around* players when they compete indoors. One reason for this is that sand-court volleyball stresses the fundamental, basic skills of the game that are essential to success in any type of volleyball. And it is those skills and the championship caliber of play found on the indoor courts and beaches of the West Coast upon which this book is based.

The Basic Skills

> *I was going up to the plate and thinking this elbow should be here and this one there and my wrist up here and my body positioned this way. I had so damn many things to think about that before I knew it, the ball was by me.*
>
> JAY JOHNSTONE,
> former California Angels outfielder

ONE OF THE KEYS to success in learning to play any sport is knowing just what to learn. Trying to learn too much can be just as disastrous as not learning enough.

Hitting a volleyball — like hitting a baseball, tennis ball, or golf ball — can become a very complicated thing, with a hundred step-by-step techniques and tips to remember. But it doesn't have to be like that.

6

This section is aimed at teaching the fundamental skills of volleyball in the simplest way possible. It's written and illustrated with the idea that it is necessary to remember only two or three good habits for most plays in volleyball. And if you learn good habits in the beginning, you shouldn't have too many bad habits to correct later on.

However, no book, including this one, will magically turn someone into a good volleyball player *without practice*. Using this book as a guide, you should look at the photographs — particularly the sequence shots — time and time again.

While practicing, look at the photos and, without a ball, (1) try to simulate the action in the sequence photos in slow motion; (2) repeat the movement at normal speed; (3) finally, repeat the movement again, this time with a ball.

A final note: While individual styles differ among volleyball players, these basic skills differ very little among the top indoor and outdoor players.

THE SERVE

The *serve* in volleyball is not the overpowering weapon it often is in tennis, but the basic idea is the same: get the ball over the net, hopefully where it will put the player receiving it at a disadvantage.

Because points are scored in volleyball only by the team that is serving, a good serve can sometimes be the difference between winning and losing.

Fig. 1–4) The floater serve: *Toss the ball gently up in front of you, then hit sharply, but not too hard, so that the ball leaves your hand without spin or rotation.*

Faulting on a serve is not only embarrassing [and, in a close game, demoralizing], but also means that your team will be playing just to keep the other team from scoring.

There are three ways to fault during the serve: (1) stepping over the back line while serving, (2) serving the ball into the net, and (3) serving the ball out of bounds or off the court.

Of the three, the first is the least excusable, particularly outdoors, where the court boundaries are usually marked with rope lines. The third — serving out of bounds — can sometimes still score a point. If the ball is served close enough to either the side or the back lines, even a good player will sometimes play the ball rather than let it fall untouched, perhaps landing inbounds.

While an out-of-bounds ball might still result in a play, a "net" ball is always just a lost serve. If the ball touches the net on the serve, even just slightly, the serve goes over to the other team.

In beach volleyball (usually played with two-man teams), most serves are delivered overhand. Similar to a baseball throw or tennis swing, the overhand delivery can be used for several types of serves.

The most effective of these is the *floater* (Fig. 1–4). Used up to about 80 percent of the time by tournament players, the floater is served sharply and without spin. Served the correct way, the floater will move erratically, dancing as unpredictably as a knuckleball pitch in baseball. (Not too surprisingly, the floater is sometimes referred to as a *knuckler*.)

The floater is an especially difficult serve to receive when it is served into the wind. Because the wind often plays an important role in beach tournaments, it's easy to understand its popularity among top players.

The floater: This should generally be a sharp serve, made with a quick wrist snap and just a brief contact between either the heel of the hand or a slightly cupped hand and the ball. Although a slow floater usually allows a player to follow its erratic movements and recover in time to receive it, a slower serve is still a good idea as a change of pace.

The knuckler effect of the floater can also be increased by serving the ball with the air valve pointed toward the opposing team. That may sound ridiculous, but there is a noticeable difference. Whether the added effect comes from wind resistance against the needle hole and stem, or because the valve stem creates a slight out-of-balance point (each theory has its supporters), the fact of the matter is that it works. And most tournament-quality players carefully position the valve stem before each serve. Depending on wind direction, the ball will break or drift in the direction in which the valve stem is pointed on a floater serve, such as a rise, drop, or break to one side. Because this drift may be just enough to prevent a serve from going out of bounds — or just enough to make it go out of bounds — it's worth practicing to see how it works best for you.

The *spin* or *roundhouse* serve (Fig. 5–9) is faster, but it is usually easier for the opposing team to play than a

(FIG. 5–9)   The roundhouse serve: *Toss the ball higher and farther above your head than in the floater serve. As the ball drops, shift your weight from your rear foot to your front foot, fully extend your arm, and snap your wrist through and over the ball to give it top spin.*

6

7

8

9

floater. A serve with spin may drop or curve, but the rotation is easy to spot, and the movement or curve is usually predictable. Most players also find it more difficult to serve a roundhouse without faulting than the floater. Like the floater, it is much more effective when served into the wind; when served hard into a strong wind, it can drop so fast that the receiving team has little time to react.

The roundhouse: In this serve, the ball is tossed higher and more directly overhead than with the floater. To get more power into the serve, the server rocks back onto his rear foot (right foot for a right-handed player) and, as the overhand arm swing begins, strides forward, shifting the weight to the front foot. Contact with the ball is made more overhead and with the arm more extended than with the floater. (Because the floater is made with a lower toss and more in front of the server, it is usually easier to control and learn.)

The wrist plays the most important part in the roundhouse. Contact with the lower rear part of the ball is made with the palm and heel of the hand — and with the wrist still cocked back. As the ball is touched, the wrist snaps forward, with the palm fingers rolling over the ball, adding the spin.

For the spectator, the most spectacular serve is the *skyball* or *highboy* (Fig. 10–15). Used frequently in beach tournaments when the sun is directly overhead, the skyball is another good change-of-pace serve. Unlike the floater

15

(FIG. 10–15)   The skyball serve: *Usually hit with a cupped palm, the skyball must be hit very high to be effective. For the most power and control, bend your knees, and, as you straighten up, swing your hand up through the bottom of the ball and follow through.*

12

13

or the roundhouse, the skyball works best when served with the wind, rather than into it. Hit as high as possible, the skyball is difficult to serve consistently with control, but it can also be difficult to receive.

The skyball: Holding the ball with his palm up, the server bends his knees, then uses a strong underhand swing as the body straightens up, providing the power for the serve. The ball is usually hit with a cupped hand. However, some players use either a fist or the heel of the thumb to hit this serve.

There are other serves used in volleyball, but the floater, the roundhouse, and the skyball are the most common and the ones most seen in tournaments.

Girls, and younger or beginning players, might find the *underhand serve* (Fig. 16–19) the easiest way to get the ball over the net. Using the fist (Fig. 17) will usually add a little more power to the serve.

A similar serve, and a favorite of some indoor players, is the *sidearm* or *international* serve (Fig. 20). This swing can be used to serve a floater-type ball, but the ball usually is served slower than the normal overhand floater. Some players, however, use a more overhead version of this same stiff-armed serve to hit a hard top-spin serve.

SERVING NOTES

As a basic rule, the placement — where the ball goes — is the most important part of the serve.

19

(FIG. 16–19)   The underhand serve: *The easiest serve to learn, the underhand is hit with either the fist or cupped palm. Simply stride forward, swinging your hand up through the ball.*

18

19

Generally, a serve on the back line is harder to play than one close to the net, simply because the first pass has to travel farther to get close to the net (where the receiving team wants to be able to play the ball).

Particularly at the start of a game, a team may have trouble playing a serve close to the back or side lines, being uncertain as to whether or not it will land out of bounds.

A serve that splits the middle between two players will often confuse both, each thinking the other will play it and each allowing it to drop. Even more effective is a serve that starts toward one player and then breaks toward the other, again going between both of them.

Where the players are positioned on the court to receive the serve will usually dictate where it should go. For example, in beach doubles, if the team has inched back to guard against the long serve, a short serve just dropping over the net is tough to play. If one player seems to be cheating toward the center of the court, a serve along the sideline may be effective.

The team receiving the serve should almost always be made to move after the serve, rather than have the ball served directly toward the players.

Serve to a team's weakness. Because beach doubles (two-man teams) is basically a game where the player receiving the ball passes it to his partner, who in turn sets the ball back to him to be spiked or hit, it makes sense to serve to the least consistent passer; or so that its weakest hitter will receive and therefore hit the ball; or so that the weakest setter will be setting the pass from his partner. (This is one reason why players should seek partners of about the same level of ability. A top spiker would probably never get a single serve in a beach tournament if he teamed with a weak hitter.)

An "ace" or serve that lands inbounds and untouched can often be the turning point in a game. If a player starts thinking about the serve he just missed, the one that is coming will be just that much harder to play.

It's easy to lose track of the score in a game. To avoid hard feelings (and lost points), it's best to make sure the score is announced before serving.

Make sure the other team is facing you and is ready before serving.

On extremely windy days, the easiest serve to receive is one with a light backspin. This is a good serve to use with beginning players and is made using the same basic serving motion as with the floater. However, a flat hand is used to slap at the rear bottom portion of the ball.

In beach doubles, the ball may be served from anywhere behind the backcourt line. (This rule may be used to advantage in certain wind conditions.) Indoors, or if there are more than two players on a beach team, the ball must be served by the player closest to the right court boundary line (on the server's right as he faces the net) and behind the righthand third (ten feet) of the back line.

A teammate cannot screen the server from the view of the opposing team. The server must be in full view of his opponents.

A tough serve will often cause the other team to accidentally bump or hit the ball back over the net on the first play. Whenever a serve is made, the server's partner or teammates should be prepared to play any ball that comes unexpectedly back over the net on the first hit.

A tough serve is a big advantage in volleyball. However, it is better to ease up a little, rather than to try to make a serve so tough (for example, close to the net or close to the back or sidelines) that it hits the net or goes out of bounds. The team that usually wins in volleyball is the team that makes the fewest mistakes — including mistakes on the serve.

Offense

OFFENSE

AFTER PLAY BEGINS with a serve, volleyball, as in most team sports, is a battle between offense and defense. In beach doubles, most of the advantages rest with the offense: it is just the opposite indoors, where defense dominates the play.

The offensive team in volleyball is *not* the serving team but the team that is receiving the serve (and then, if the ball continues in play, whichever team has the ball). However, if the receiving team can make a good "pass," a good "set," and a good "hit," the chances are good that it will score a "sideout" and earn the serve (and the opportunity to see how it can do on defense).

Particularly in top beach doubles matches, where two-man teams play on a full-size court, sideouts are frequent, with the serving team's being unable to defense

25

(FIG. 20)   The international serve: *Hit with much the same swing as a tennis forearm, this serve is usually made with a cupped hand at shoulder or head level. Toss the ball out in front of you (as you face parallel to the net) and then swing with a straight, stiff arm sideways through the ball. This serve may also be used with a more overhand delivery for a serve similar to the roundhouse.*

(FIG. 21)   *The most important skill in volleyball is passing. Greg Lee,*
former UCLA basketball star and a top beach volleyball player, keeps his
eyes on the ball as he moves to keep the ball directly in front of himself—a
key to consistent passing. (PHOTO: GATHERUM)

the other team's first spike.

Both on the beach and indoors, the turning point in a rally often comes on the defensive play that allows a team to recover and finish out play with its own set and hit.

THE PASS

> *The most important play in volleyball? It's got to be the pass. Sometimes a team that's strong at the net – spiking and blocking – can overcome weaker passing. But it's rare.*
>
> RUDY SUWARA

The first offensive play — receiving the serve and passing it to a teammate who, in turn, sets the ball for the hit — is the key to the offense.

In the pass-set-hit of offense, a mistake with the beginning pass usually causes trouble throughout the sequence. And in a close match, the mistakes usually make the difference between victory and defeat.

Even the best spikers must have a good set to hit well, and the best insurance for a good set is a good, easy-to-play pass. That's why most volleyball teams serve to the weakest passer on the opposing team — hoping that a bad pass will force a weak set and hit.

The *bump*, or two-arm pass, is probably the most important of all volleyball skills (Fig. 22–24). If a player cannot pass the ball well, his team's entire offense is likely to suffer.

28

(FIG. 22–24) The bump pass: *Keeping your arms straight and elbows locked, keep low and* lift *up your arms instead of swinging up at the ball.* Some players find the lifting motion comes more naturally if they shrug their shoulders forward as contact is made.

25

(FIG. 25)   *The two-arm bump is used not only for passing, but also for most defensive digs. On a hard-hit spike (note the flattened ball), the defensive player should play the ball on the same part of the arm—the forearm—for the dig as for the normal bump pass that is used for receiving the serve.*
(PHOTO: BOB VAN WAGNER)

The bump is used not only to receive the serve, but also sometimes as a way to set the ball for a hit, and occasionally to make a shot over the net when a good hit is impossible and the main concern is just making sure the ball gets over the net.

The bump is used almost exclusively to receive the serve because, under modern volleyball rules, a player who receives a serve with his hands is likely to be called for a violation for mishandling the ball.

One main difference between droopy net "jungle ball" and volleyball as it is played correctly indoors or on the beach is that good players almost *always* use the bump to receive the serve, while in the jungle-ball game the ball is nearly always hit with the hands and often hit back over the net on the first hit.

Actually the bump pass is fairly easy to learn — probably the easiest of all the basic skills for the beginning player to learn.

The bump: The key to a good bump pass is a lifting motion, rather than a swinging or hitting motion with the arms.

The player's hands should be folded into one another (Fig. 26), and the arms kept straight with the elbows *locked*, so that the ball makes contact with the flat surface of the inner wrist and forearm. If your arms are correctly extended, as you contact the ball, your shoulders should be in a "shrugging" position. Some players find it helpful to "point" or bend their hands toward the ground to make sure that their elbows are locked.

32

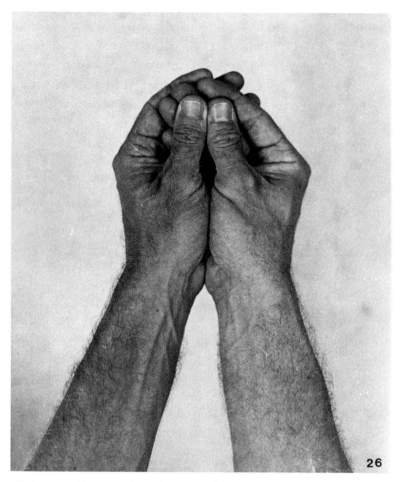

(FIG. 26)   *Positioning of the hands and fingers is a key factor in consistent passing with the two-arm bump. By placing the hands as shown here, with the thumbs together, a relatively flat surface is maintained. If the ball accidently contacts the hands (instead of the forearms) there is still a chance that a playable pass will result.*

Properly executed, the bump is almost a slow-motion movement, used to cushion the impact of the ball, with the player letting the natural bounce of the ball provide most of the height of the pass, and using the *lifting* motion of the arms and body to provide control and direction.

The one instruction constantly repeated in nearly every sport with a ball cannot be emphasized enough in volleyball: *Keep your eyes on the ball!* You should watch it while you are making any play (such as a bump), all the way through the play, including the follow-through motion.

Like a shortstop, you should always move to keep the ball directly in front of you. The most common passing mistake is a failure to move so that a normal, straight-ahead bump pass can be made. *Move your feet!* If a serve is dropping just short of where you are playing, move a step or two forward so you can make the pass without stretching. If the ball is coming off to one side, try to move behind it rather than just waiting and playing it off to one side. The most consistent pass, and the easiest to control, is the one made straight ahead.

One way to check if the bump is being executed properly is to watch the spin on the ball as it comes off your arms. The ball, bumped correctly, should have little or no spin. Usually spin is an indication you are swinging your arms too much, rather than lifting them with the elbows locked.

The bump pass should generally be made straight ahead

(FIG. 27)   *Fred Zuelich makes a bump set for his partner, Bobby Jackson, to hit during the 1973 Manhattan Open. The bump set offers good control (and little chance of a foul), and should be used when you are unable to position yourself under a pass in time to set a ball with your hands.* (PHOTO: DEWEY SCHURMAN)

on the serve reception indoors. In beach doubles, the pass should be made to *lead* the setter as he moves toward the net. (Some beach players still tend to pass more or less straight ahead, while others pass more toward the center of the court. In each case, you should be a few feet back from the net to allow enough room for the setter to make his play.)

> *The two most important parts of volleyball are the pass and the set – in that order. Over the years, the teams that put the ball on top of the net win, and not necessarily the big hitters. Even the smaller guys can put the ball away when it's on the net. Guys like Spike Boarts and Bob Hogan, who weren't big, always did well because they could pass and set to get the ball on the net.*
>
> RON LANG

The *bump set*, as the term implies, is a set made with a bump (Fig. 27).

The bump set is used when the player making the set cannot reach the pass in time to get positioned underneath to make the set.

The better players have great control over the bump and can use it almost as effectively as a set made with the hands. And there are times that the bump is the only way to set the ball.

Here are a few of the occasions when the bump set should be used:

    1. When the pass is too low (or out of reach) to allow the setter to use his hands.

36

28

(FIG. 28) *Whenever you are in trouble and have to chase the ball to make a play, the bump is usually the best and safest play to make. As Bobby Jackson demonstrates, the bump can be made from almost any angle, including directly back over your head.* (PHOTO: SCHURMAN)

2. If the pass is too high, or spinning too quickly, to set comfortably with the hands. This often happens when a defensive player "digs" a spike, giving a teammate a chance to set the ball for a hit by his own team.

3. When the pass either hits the net or is so close to the net that a setter doesn't have room to make the play unless he uses his arms for a bump set.

The bump set is made basically the same way as the bump pass. However, because the bump set is often made close to the net, the idea is often to make the ball go almost straight up in the air (just like any other set that can be hit). To direct the ball upward for a bump set, it's necessary to hold your arms more parallel to the ground than in the normal bump pass. Again, *lifting* is the most important part of the movement.

When playing the ball out of the net, the most important thing to remember is to get low, sometimes down on your knees, in order to play the ball as it drops off the net. A ball hit hard into the lower part of a taut net will often rebound back a few feet, but generally the ball will drop after hitting the net. Remember, it is easier to play the ball after it drops off the net than when it is still net high.

The bump is almost always used to receive balls that come over the net, including soft hits and "oversets" (a set that carries over the net onto the court of the defensive team).

When chasing a wild pass, or going after the ball after a

38

hard spike has been defensively "dug," it's often necessary to bump the ball back over your head to keep it in play. Even when it is made on the run, this bump is made with the same techniques of the normal bump pass — keep your arms straight, elbows locked, etc. (Fig. 28).

Even a ball that comes high, or off to one side, should be bumped whenever possible for better control.

Again, keeping your arms straight and elbows locked is the best guarantee for a good pass.

The *bump over* is a bump used to play the ball over the net.

While a ball that is bumped over is fairly easy for the other team to play, there are times when the offensive team has no other choice than to do it in order to keep the ball in play. Often the bump over is the result of a bad pass or a defensive dig that causes a desperation save on the second shot, thus forcing the use of the bump over on the third and final touch.

When a player is in "trouble" (hustling to make a saving play), the bump over is a good shot because it seldom results in a foul and allows enough control to insure that the ball will land inbounds on the other side.

The bump over is just about the only shot that can be used when the third and final shot a team has must be made from far back in the court.

Seldom is the bump over much of an offensive threat, but it will keep a rally going, giving the other team a chance to make a mistake.

29

(FIG. 29–31) The set: *Keep your hands up and ready while you move underneath the ball. Then spread your fingers (keeping them relaxed) and take the ball, just above your eyes, with the first three fingers and thumb of each hand simultaneously and* flip *the wrists forward as the arms straighten.*

30

31

(FIG. 32) *You should look through a "little window" formed by both thumbs and index fingers as you prepare to touch the ball for a set. The actual spread between the hands varies slightly among better setters. If the ball becomes wet or slippery because of sweat on the leather, you can gain better control (with less chance of mishandling the ball) by moving your hands a bit closer together.*

THE SET

The set is the soft touch in volleyball.

A setter can be compared to a basketball guard who lofts a high pass to a center for a slam dunk.

In six-man indoor volleyball, where the blocking is the key to the defense, the setter tries to find the "open" man who can avoid the block and put the ball away with a spike.

It's a different story in beach doubles. The block isn't used as often on the beach, so the setter's main concern is not so much trying to hide from the defense where he is going to set the ball, but rather simply to put up a nice soft set that can be spiked by his partner.

The *set*, in contrast to the bump, is probably the most difficult of all volleyball skills to perfect. The good set looks deceptively easy to make, but requires good hands and good timing and lots of practice (Fig. 29–31).

The fingers play the key role in the set. To make a set, comfortably spread your fingers and form a "little window" using your thumbs as the base and your index fingers (Fig. 32).

The ball should be taken with the fingers and thumb simultaneously, right at the eyes, and then pushed firmly but gently, as the arms straighten and the wrist flips forward (Fig. 33–34).

What has to be avoided at all costs is stiffness. Stiff fingers will often result in a "throw" or violation for a mishandled ball.

(FIG. 33–34)   *The wrist flip is the key to a soft set. If the fingers are relaxed, the ball should leave the hands with little or no spin as the wrists rotate forward.*

(FIG. 35) *Jumping to confuse the defense, Toshi Toyoda (No. 3) delivers a quick, low (just above the net) set to a teammate who is also already in the air. This type of fast, deceptive offense is the trademark of the modern game, designed to outmaneuver the defense. Here, the play has worked so well that the opposing blocker is caught flatfooted on the floor.* (PHOTO: VAN WAGNER)

For a long or high set, the setter should bend his knees and push off with his legs to add power to the set.

The difference between making a good clean set and a mishandled ''throw'' takes times and experience. In the rulebooks the throw is described as a ball that comes visibly to rest, but in practice there is wide variation.

Nearly all players agree that the call has always been more strictly enforced on the beach than in indoor play.

Among tournament beach players, most sets leave the setter's hands with little or no spin. If there is too much, a throw is usually called on the assumption that it did not come out of the hands cleanly.

Passes that are received by the setter off to the side of his body (rather than at his forehead), or too low (say, below his chin), are also considered throws because it's almost impossible to take a ball that way and set it cleanly without having it stop or come to rest in the hands.

Actually the most common setting mistake is the failure to *move to* the pass quickly enough so that, positioned under the ball and facing the direction the set is to be made, you can set easily, without having to ''force'' the placement of the set.

It's best to face exactly the direction you're going to set (especially in doubles) because that is the best way to control the placement of the set. Setting off to the side, rather than straight ahead, should be left to experienced setters.

If there is no referee, the throw is an honor call left up to the judgment of the individual players. Usually, as a

46

player's setting improves, his opinion of what constitutes a throw becomes more critical, and he's liable to call "throws" on sets he would have previously let go.

In beach play, the setter must generally be facing the direction in which he sets — that is, the ball should be set directly in front of him. A set that is pushed off toward the left or right, away from directly in front of him, is usually regarded as a throw on the beach. However, indoors there is a tendency to allow more leniency on this call, and a setter will sometimes seem to "carry" the ball in changing direction so that the set goes off to the side of his body rather than straight ahead. (See "Rules and Referees," pp. 102–121.)

In both beach and indoor play, the back set is legal, although it is used much more often indoors as a means to deceive the blockers. On the beach, it is usually used only when the setter has to chase a pass and finds himself with his back to the net or his partner. However, because it is more difficult to set back over your head, most players are better off using the bump set in this situation. The same rules apply to the back set as to the normal set, and the ball should come off the hands cleanly and directly in back of the setter, not off to one side.

Every setter should know where his teammates like the ball set for a hit. It is one of the first things you should ask someone you are playing with for the first time.

On the beach, where the block is not used as frequently, the ball should ideally be set so close to the net that it would just graze it if allowed to fall. Because the sand cuts down a player's jump by four or more inches, it's necessary to set the ball close to the net for most players to spike the ball down at a sharp angle. If the ball is set back from the net — unless the spiker is a great jumper — the spike cannot be hit down without its going into the net.

Indoors, a ball set too close to the net is easier to block. And because you can jump higher off a hardwood floor than off sand, the ball is usually set about two feet back from the net.

The setter also has to learn whether the spiker likes a high or a low set. Indoors, where wind is not a factor, the high set was the standard until the 1964 Olympics, when the Japanese displayed their fast offense based in part on quick sets just a foot or two above the net. These low sets left the defense no time to react or set a block. On the beach, the high set (though not quite as high as indoors) is still the favorite of most good hitters, although as the wind increases, most players tend to keep their sets lower for more control.

A setter has to be mature, intelligent . . . be able to think about the other team's defense, the block, where his hitters are, which of his hitters are not free, and how to free them – all while he's making the set.

RUDY SUWARA

48

Ron Lang, one of the game's premier setters, was asked recently why he now sometimes makes a set with his hands low (at his chin, rather than at his eyes). "I don't get there [under the pass] now," he said. "It's a matter of being lazy."

One of the most consistent setters in beach volleyball is Ron Von Hagen, who doesn't have what players call "really nice hands." He is not the picture-perfect setter. However, his sets are easy to hit and he is one of the favorite setters of a host of top beach hitters. What makes Von Hagen a top setter is that he never lets up on hustle. If a pass is within reach, Von Hagen is virtually certain to be camped under the ball when it comes down, ready to make a good set. It's hard to make a good set with your hands if you are not stable. If you can't get under the pass to set it with your hands, it's better to bump set the ball.

Hitting

THE SPIKE IS what put the "power" in *power volleyball*, as the modern game is sometimes called. The spike, which occurs when a player leaps high above the net to smash a softly set ball down into the opponents' court, is not an easy play to make for most players; it requires both strong jumping ability and good timing.

A well-hit spike is the game's strongest offensive weapon (spiked balls have been clocked at upward of a hundred miles an hour), and modern volleyball offense has been built around the spike, and the defense around ways to try to stop it.

Volleyball, like basketball, has been called a "big man's game." The reason is the spike. The average height for a man in the United States is under six feet, but even most six-footers cannot reach the top of an eight-foot volleyball net.

On the beach, you lose at least four to six inches in height on a jump owing to the soft sand, so spiking is even more difficult. But defensive blocking indoors more than makes up for the difference. Indoors or outdoors, the taller the spiker, the better chance he has of hitting an effective spike.

Basketball players, with their height and jumping ability, have traditionally made strong volleyball players.

UCLA, a powerhouse in both basketball and volleyball, has had a number of players who have been outstanding in both sports. Keith Erickson, a star with the Los Angeles Lakers and the Phoenix Suns, played both basketball and volleyball at UCLA and helped lead the U.S. volleyball team in the 1964 Olympics. He was also one of the outstanding spikers in beach volleyball for years.

John Vallely and Greg Lee, who were playmakers on NCAA championship basketball squads at UCLA in recent years, are also considered among the best of the AAA-rated beach players.

Two years ago, Wilt Chamberlain took up volleyball. He has used his seven-foot height to great advantage in both spiking and blocking in beach tournaments, as well as on tour with his indoor volleyball team, the Big Dippers.

Still, you don't have to be tall to be a good hitter: Toshi Toyoda, a five-foot-seven All American volleyballer for UCLA, spikes well enough both indoors and on the beach

51

(FIG. 36–41)   The spike: *Wait for the set about three strides
back from the net. Then, as the ball is set, stay low and move
quickly toward the ball, plant both feet together, crouch and use
your armswing to jump as high as possible. It's most important
to remember to always* stay behind *the ball on the hit, so that
you can extend your arm and make contact with the ball out in
front of you. Running under the ball is probably the most
common error beginning players make in the hit.*

38

39

40

41

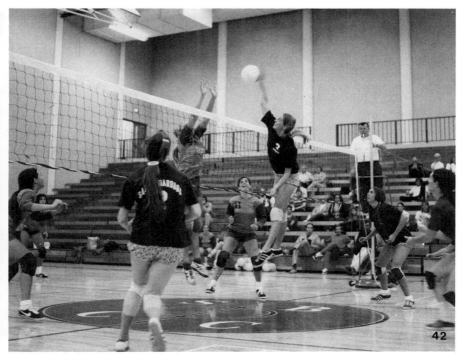

(FIG. 42) *Lisa Richards, of the UCSB women's volleyball team, shows the importance of a fully extended arm for added reach when spiking—particularly when hitting over the block.* (PHOTO: GATHERUM)

to be considered one of the better all-around players in the game.

Some coaches have called the *spike* one of the most difficult and demanding maneuvers in sports (Fig. 37–41).

The most frequent error beginning players make in trying to spike is running underneath the ball. Basketball players, who are used to positioning themselves under a rebound, have an especially hard time trying to break the habit while spiking.

By running under the set, rather than just about two feet behind it, you are forced to look up at the ball while hitting it. This not only prevents you from seeing what the defense is doing, but also won't allow you to spike down on the ball, which you can do when the ball is out in front of you.

The spike is really not much more than a run, jump, and swing. Some players who are natural athletes never have much trouble with the spike. Others, even though they learn the other basic skills of the game well enough, never quite seem to get the knack of spiking consistently.

If you have difficulty learning to spike well, check the following tips to see if you can find something that will improve your spiking.

1. After making the pass, *wait* about three full strides back from the net and watch *where* the set is going. Do not commit yourself by moving to where you *think* the set will be.

(FIG. 43)   *The dink is the spiker's change-up. Henry Bergmann is shown as he starts to dink just over the outstretched hands of the opposing blockers. To be effective, the hitter must look until the last possible moment like he is going to spike the ball.* (PHOTO: GATHERUM)

(FIG. 44)　*Against a two-man UCLA block, Henry Bergmann leaps high to hit a hard spike down the line. Most players tend to hit spikes at a crosscourt angle, as evidenced by the position of the blockers.* (PHOTO: GATHERUM)

2. After you see where the set is going, *run hard and low* toward the ball — *but do not run underneath it*. As high jumpers have learned, generally the faster you move toward the bar, the higher you will be able to jump. If you are too close to the net or run underneath the set, you have to jump without a running start. If you start more than about three strides back from the net, timing the jump and hit becomes more difficult.

3. After moving to the set, *plant both feet* together and *crouch low*. Jumping off only one foot (a common basketball habit) results in a considerable loss of jumping height, particularly in the sand. By crouching low, you will avoid the habit most people have of jumping without really getting low enough to bring the muscles of the thighs and buttocks into play. These muscles are what provides the spring in the jump.

4. As you jump, *swing* your arms up for added lift, and then jump *straight* up. Do not "broadjump" toward the net; jumping forward means you are losing valuable inches in height.

5. As your arms swing up, *cock* your hitting hand behind your ear and then swing, *fully extending* your arm. If you are an extremely good jumper, it's possible to hit with a bit more power by hitting with an arm that is *slightly* bent rather than fully extended. But most players are far better off extending their arms so that the ball can be hit at the fullest extent of the reach.

59

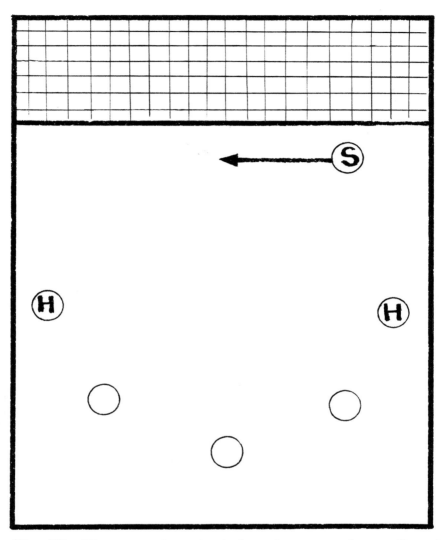

(FIG. 45) *The crescent formation is the easiest way to play an offense in a game in which not all of the players are experienced. Used with from three to six players on a team, this crescent is formed by the players receiving the serve. Whatever the number of players, the ball is passed to the middle of the court near the net for the setter, who sets to either of the other two frontline hitters. With four players on a team, there would be one player in the back row (instead of three as shown here) with the two hitters and setter remaining in the positions in which they are shown in the diagram.*

6. In the spike, as well as in every other volleyball skill,
keep your eyes on the ball throughout the entire run,
jump, and swing.

> *When I first started, I didn't have a dink. I just got
> up and swung.*
>
> RON LANG

As with a pitcher who tries to get by with only a fastball,
even the strongest hitters will find the defense can ''dig''
his spikes if the spike is the only shot he has. The soft *dink*
tapped just over the net (or, if there is a block, just over
the blocker's hands) is the equivalent of the pitcher's
changeup. It makes the spike just that much more effective
(Fig. 44).

To fool the defense, which is usually set for a hard
spike, you must disguise your intention to make the soft
shot. You should approach the ball the same as you would
for a spike, jump the same way, and then only at the last
possible moment lightly touch the ball with your fist or
heel of your hand. Indoors, a dink with the fingertips is
allowed.

On the beach, it is important that the ball does not come
to a stop in your hand or a ''throw'' will be called.
Indoors, referees have shown more leniency in the call and
have allowed players to almost catch the ball on their
fingertips and then ''carry'' it to guide its direction on a
dink.

Another play off the dink is the *long dink*. This is really

61

a fake dink in which you look like you are going to dink just over the net and, as the defensive players move up to cover it, you give the ball a short, hard tap so that it goes over their heads — hopefully landing just inside the back line.

The third basic shot for the hitter is the *cut shot*.

The idea of this shot is to hit the ball just over the net and nearly parallel to it. In other words, it is a sort of dink that travels from one far edge of the court to the other.

Although some of the best spikers hit this shot quite hard, it is commonly hit not much harder than a dink. Again, to make the shot effective, you should make it appear as if you are going to hit a normal spike. At the last instant, you slow your armswing and flip your wrist so that you hit the side of the ball, sending it just over and down along the net.

Although most beginning players find it easier to make this shot hitting from the right side (if they are right-handed), it does not take long to learn how to make the shot from either side of the court.

Most beginning players fall into habits regarding where they hit the ball. If you always hit the ball to the same spots, it won't take long for the defense to figure out how and where to play you. To be a good hitter, you have to learn how to move the ball around with a variety of shots. This is especially true of the shorter player who needs an almost perfect set to spike hard.

62

One way for a hitter to use a blocker to his advantage is to hit the ball so that it glances off his hands with enough force to carry it out of bounds. This technique takes time to learn, but it is one that is necessary for an indoor player to learn to be an effective spiker.

Hit into the wind, a hard hit with topspin (like the roundhouse serve) will drop suddenly and usually land inbounds. This is a good shot to use when the set is back from the net, preventing you from making a normal spike.

A set that is back from the net also limits other shots. For example, if the set is six to eight feet back from the net, a dink takes so long to travel to the net that a defensive player has time to react and make a play before it hits the court. The same holds true for a cut shot.

Similarly, the best time to use a dink or cut shot is on a good set, when the defense would least expect it. On the beach, a set that is right on top of the net (not a few feet back) is the best set for a dink as well as a spike. If the set is also outside (near the side of the court), it is also the best set for a cut shot.

> *You can't really look* [as you go up to hit] to see where the defense is, because you'll probably hit the ball into the net. But you can look a little out of the corner of your eye — more at the movement than anything else.
>
> HENRY BERGMANN

Most spikers (assuming they are right-handed) would rather make an approach straight to the net when hitting on the right side (when facing the net). If the ball is set more

(FIG. 46)   *Indoors as well as on the beach, the basic digging position is the same as is used for the bump pass. Here, Bruno Andriukaitus, of the Chicago-based Kenneth Allen Volleyball Club, prepares to dig a spike in the backcourt that was just hit crosscourt inside the block of his teammate, Gordon Lindstrom (No. 31).* (PHOTO: VAN WAGNER)

toward the middle of the court, the right-side hitter should move toward the center of the court and then move straight toward the net for the hit. Coming in at an angle (from the outside toward the center of the court) when playing on the right side will prevent the spiker from hitting the ball straight down the right sideline, unless he has tremendous wrist control.

At the same time, most spikers playing the left side (facing the net) prefer to approach the ball from an angle, sometimes even from outside the court, because that offers the best angle to make a strong cross court shot.

THE CRESCENT

It's a good idea, especially in pickup volleyball games in which some of the players may not be too experienced, to have a simple offense so that everyone isn't running into one another.

The simplest offense, which can be used by any team with from three to six players on a side, is sometimes called the *crescent*. In this offense, the serve is received by any one of the players in the crescent, who passes it to the setter stationed near the net, who in turn sets it for one of the two outside hitters.

If there are only three players on a side, the setter — staying by the net and blocking on defense — will set to either of his two teammates. If there are four, five, or six players on a team, only the outside hitters (because they are closest to the net in the crescent pattern and are therefore considered the front-row players along with the setter) will do the hitting (Fig. 45).

In this offense, a different player becomes the setter with each rotation. In organized team play, it is not very efficient to have every player (even the weaker setters) doing the setting, but in friendly pickup games, it insures that everyone will have the chance to both set and spike.

The key to playing this type of game is to let the setter always make the second touch (which should be a set) by his team.

On both serves and defense, the setter should let a teammate make the first play or touch. Unless there is a wild pass, the setter should then be able to set the ball for either of the two hitters.

On the defense, if the setter does not touch the ball on the block, he should land and turn quickly to see if one of his teammates managed to get the ball into the air. If so, the setter should be able to make the set.

If the setter touches the ball on the block, that of course leaves only two hits to get the ball back over the net. In that case, the second player to make a touch should, if possible, try to set the ball for a spike on the last hit.

FOR THE GIRLS

The difference between men's and women's volleyball is, in a word, strength.

66

Most women lack the necessary strength in their arms and legs to become powerful spikers, despite the lower net (7 feet 4½ inches) used in women's play.

Dixie Grimmett, who coached her Cal State Long Beach women's team to a national championship in 1973, said that except for the fact that men's volleyball is more physical, men and women play the game the same way. Her team, for example, uses the same advanced 6–0 (three-hitter) attack used by the powerhouse men's team at Long Beach, which finished runner-up to San Diego State in the 1973 NCAA championships.

Chris Accornero, women's volleyball coach at UCSB, says that motivation seems to be what separates the men from the women in collegiate volleyball. "You can usually get the guys to throw their bodies on the floor after a ball without coaxing. With girls, you always have to encourage them to give that 100 percent effort."

She also points out that defensive alignments are sometimes slightly different for the girls, since men usually spike the ball down at a sharper angle. However, as Dixie Grimmett notes, men are also blocking higher, so that women's spikes — except for the power and speed — should be defensed by the same positioning as those by men.

Although women sometimes seem less aggressive than men in volleyball, the setting and defense of women's play can reach high standards. Setting, requiring a soft touch as well as coordination, is a skill that many girls pick up faster than men.

67

Nationally, women's competition, like the men's, is dominated by West Coast teams. The exceptions are few, such as the 1972 National Women's Championship team, E Pluribus Unum from Texas, whose coach, Mary Jo Peppler, was a transplant from the West Coast.

However, anyone who has seen the Japanese National women's team in action can testify to the fact that women can play a brand of power volleyball equal to men's for speed and excitement.

Defense

DEFENSE

The biggest luxury in the game is defense. In order of importance, it's way down the line after passing, setting, hitting, even the serve .... But it's nice if you have it.

RON LANG

YOU MIGHT TAKE that statement with a grain of salt, as it comes from the man generally regarded as the top defensive player in beach volleyball for more than fifteen years. For the most part, he's probably right — but only on the beach.

Indoors there is a premium on defense, which, because of the block, can account for the majority of a team's points. However, in beach doubles, more points come from a team's mistakes in passing and setting than from defensive brilliance. Still, a strong defensive play, particularly on a hard spike, can sap the morale of the other team faster than any other play in volleyball.

Ron Lang remembers the turning point in a match in the 1967 Santa Barbara Open as being two defensive plays: ''I remember digging [Larry] Rundle on two of his hardest hits in about five minutes . . . . Both times he smashed the ball straight down, and both times it shot back over his head. He later admitted that it had hurt him mentally.''

But Lang says, ''It's like that sometimes on defense. You just put out an arm and it happens. Sometimes everything you touch comes up.''

The key to good defense on the beach is keeping your body low to the ground so you can react faster toward the ball, as well as *being in the right place at the right time*. With just two players attempting to cover the same ground as six players cover indoors, there is little margin for error. It's a fact that usually forces beach players to become top defensive players.

Against the average or beginning beach player, defense is generally a matter of positioning yourself where the hitter usually hits. For example, most beginning players, whether hitting from the right or left side, usually hit most of their shots at a cross court angle. Some will virtually hit every good set to the same spot, using a dink or cut shot only when the set is poor.

Defense is a different story entirely against the better sand-court players.

Just as basketball great Bob Cousy could be driving toward the hoop and still spot, and pass to, an open teammate in a crowd of defenders, a top beach player can spike to open areas by "seeing" the defense with peripheral vision at the same time he's in midair, watching the ball he's going to hit. However, in a crucial situation, even better players will usually go to their strongest shot — in volleyball as well as basketball.

Most beach tournament players have watched and played against one another for years, so a Ron Lang will have a good idea where a Henry Bergmann or Larry Rundle will hit.

And it can work the other way. In 1967, Lang noticed that Rundle had developed a habit of playing defense against his cross court spike by always covering the same hitting channel. By hitting the ball to different areas rather than the easier percentage shot that Rundle was always covering, Lang said he was able to bother Rundle's whole defense.

Against better players, defense is not just a matter of trying to take away an opponent's best shot by covering it and forcing him to hit somewhere else. Because the top players can "move around" their shots (hitting to different parts of the court), it usually becomes necessary to, as Bergmann says, "show them one place, and then go to another."

What that means is that, as the player starts to commit himself with his armswing on the spike, you should move from where you are on defense to another spot you think he will try to hit instead. It's not all guesswork because top defensive players such as Bergmann or Lang can "read"

71

(Fig. 47)   *Kirk Kilgour, right, who raced close to the net to guard against a
spike hit sharply downward by Bobby Jackson, puts his hands up to play the
ball. Kilgour's partner, Doug Dunlap, who is playing farther back, keeps his
hands down in the basic bump-dig position.* (PHOTO: SCHURMAN)

the angle a hitter approaches the ball, the direction his body faces, or the way he starts his armswing, and know that he is going to hit the ball straight in front of him or crosscourt.

That kind of knowledge comes only with experience. But once you begin to know where your opponents tend to hit their spikes, you can begin to play better defense. However, if you wait until you are in a game before thinking about where to play a hitter, you can be crucial points behind before your defense starts to click. You should always make a habit of watching other players to see where they hit.

If you can scout the teams you're going to play in a tournament by watching them in early matches, you'll have an immediate advantage at the start of the game. Also, while your opponents are warming up and hitting practice spikes, watch again to see where their shots are going.

But, being in the right place is only half the battle.

The block is the cornerstone of indoors defense, but "digs" are as important indoors as on the beach. The basic digging position is the same as for the bump pass (Fig. 46).

Unless a player is spiking down at a sharp angle, most hard hits will land in the back half of the court. This is particularly true indoors, where the block usually prevents a spiker from hitting straight down.

You can generally base your defense midway back in the court. Stationed there, and by readying yourself for a

73

48

(FIG. 48)   *Rudy Suwara plays an overset during a beach tournament. An overset is a ball that accidentally drifts over the net on the set, but often lands untouched because the defense fails to see that the ball is going to come over, and is expecting a hard spike by the hitter. Here, Suwara ignored a fake swing at the ball by the spiker and was able to play the ball. The same low-to-the-ground bump position is also used to play balls out of the net.* (PHOTO: SCHURMAN)

dig with your arms down and out in front of you, you are prepared to dig a ball hit in front of you by bumping it. You have more control playing balls hit sharply to one side by using both arms with the bump-dig technique. However, the only play available on some extremely hard-hit balls that leave time only to react is just to stick out your arm for a one-arm dig.

One reason Bergmann prefers to play the left side of the court (facing the net) is because he feels more comfortable on defense with his ''best'' hand (he's right-handed) in the middle of the court where most shots are hit. By being halfway back in the court, you can let most hard-hit balls at head level or higher go past, because they will usually be out of bounds. This is, again, a judgment that comes with experience.

The key to knowing when to play in the back half of the court on defense, and when to move closer to the net, is the set. If a set is about three or more feet back from the net, only an exceptional hitter will be able to hit the ball down at an angle. So, if you see that a set is back, you should remain in the back half of the court. Even if your opponent should try to dink the ball just over the net, you should still have enough time to make a play because the hitter is also back from the net.

On the other hand, in beach volleyball, if the ball is set close to the net, you also have to move closer to the net — especially against a good spiker (Fig. 47).

Not only is a good spiker likely to hit a set that is ''on top of the net'' straight down on the beach, but there is also

75

(FIG. 49–50)   *Two views of the front dive. In Fig. 49, Henry Bergmann shows the proper way to bump a ball on a dive. In Fig. 50, Larry Rundle prepares to land on the floor and slide after bumping the ball with the back of his right hand. Chance of injury on a dive is lessened if you stay low and dive low to the ground.* (PHOTO: GATHERUM)

the possibility that the set will drift over the net (Fig. 48). An overset is a mistake that the defensive team should be able to turn to their advantage. However, allowing an overset to land untouched because you were playing too far back in the court on defense is a mistake that will cost you a point or a sideout every time.

When you do move closer to the net on defense in beach volleyball, you should move low to the ground, with your hands about shoulder high. With your hands up, you have a better chance to dig the ball hit straight down at you by a good spiker. Because a hard spike travels at ninety to one hundred miles an hour (about as fast as a tennis serve or a major-league fastball) and because you may be only a few feet away from the ball when it's hit, defense close to the net is almost all reflex.

Indoors, there is much less "free-lancing" on defense. Blocking forces the spiker to hit the ball in "channels" away from the block. Because these channels are predictable, defensive strategy for a six-man indoor team can be diagramed much the same way as for a football team.

For the player, it is a fact of life that the game is played indoors on a hard, wooden floor. This is the factor that makes some of the individual indoor defensive skills different from those of the beach.

Nobody likes to get "strawberries," or scrapes, from sliding across a wood floor, so it is not surprising that, until about 1964, diving for the ball was never very popular in indoor volleyball.

What revolutionized indoor defense was the play of

Japan's women's team in the 1964 Olympics in Tokyo.

Stressing defensive skills, Coach Hirofumi Diamatsu had the team practice after their normal workday, for eight hours or more every day of the week. He ran exhausting drills that forced the girls to dive after the ball in all directions, roll over, and be ready instantly to make another diving dig.

The result was a defensive team that virtually refused to let any hit, spike, or dink land untouched. It was enough to win the gold medal.

Diving on defense has now become a standard technique for all indoor teams.

There are two basic dive techniques. In the *front dive*, you dive forward, bump the ball with both forearms (or, if you can barely reach the ball, with the back of your hand) while you are in the air, then cushion your landing with your hands and pull yourself into a slide on your uniform to help ease the shock (Fig. 49–50).

The *side dive* is taken from the Japanese. You begin by staying low to the ground (as you should on defense at all times), then push yourself toward the ball as it passes to one side. As you dig the ball with one arm, you roll over and come back to your feet (Fig. 51–53). On both dives, and in indoor play in general, wearing knee pads will help protect you against floor burns.

The basic idea of defense is the same in beach doubles as in the six-man indoors game: *Get the ball into the air!*

If you can make a dig and put the ball in the air where your teammate can reach it, you're one-third of the way through the pass-set-hit offense.

If the ball is hit at you, your reflexes and positioning will determine whether you will make contact with the ball.

However, it is just as important to react if the ball is hit away from you. If your partner or teammate manages to dig the ball so that it just barely gets up (or so that it caroms off at a wild angle), your only hope is that you have been anticipating, and reaching in time to get to the ball to make a set — or, at least, to make a play that will keep the ball in the air so it can possibly be hit over the net on the third hit.

THE BLOCK

In the last few years, with players getting bigger and jumping higher, the block has come to be used more on the beach. Most beach players, however, still only use it the way football teams use a blitz or "red dog" on defense.

Because reaching over the net on a block is not allowed on the beach (although it is indoors), the beach player is at a disadvantage in blocking. But blocking sometimes becomes a necessity on the sand because a team is setting and hitting so well that the block may be the only weapon left to disrupt it.

The best set to hit, as has been explained earlier, is a set right on top of the net. And likewise, the best set to block is the same one — so close to the net that the blocker can almost touch it without reaching over.

79

51

(FIG. 51–53)   *The side dive and roll is used when you have to reach to make a one-arm bump. Staying low, you should contact the ball, then let your momentum carry you onto your back, rolling over into a ready position. Both the side and front dives should be practiced on mats at first.*

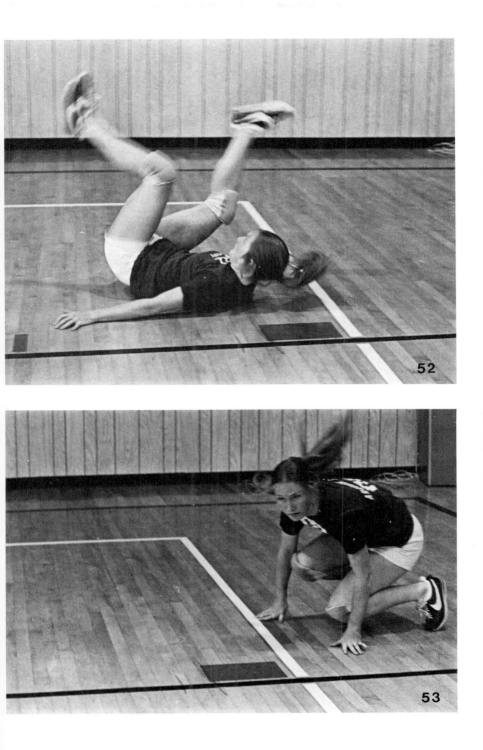

52

53

(Fig. 54) *A quick "one set" to the middle hitter in a three-hitter offense must be timed perfectly, with the hitter already in the air when the setter releases the set just above the net. Ready to react as the play develops is Rudy Suwara, one of the best indoor blockers in the U.S.* (PHOTO: GATHERUM)

If a team is setting the ball consistently on top of the net, and if the hitter is consistently putting the ball away with a hard spike because of it, it is a good idea to block at least some of the time. Even if the block is not successful, the possibility of the block may bother the hitter on the next play. Also, the setter may try to keep the ball back a little farther from the net. Either way, it helps the defense.

Indoors, blockers are allowed to reach over the net. Consequently, the setter must always keep the ball back about two or three feet from the net or it will be "stuffed" by the blocker. (The one problem many top indoor players have when they play on the beach is trying to break the habit of reaching over the net on a block.)

The block, like the spike, requires a strong jump. But unlike the spiker, the blocker does not get a chance to use a two- or three-step approach and a full armswing for a maximum jump. (Only players in the front line may block. Blocks cannot be made by players coming from the back row.) Because a blocker must be ready to *react* defensively, depending on where the ball is set for the hit, you should keep low, with your hands up.

The closer to the net you are when blocking, the more effective your block will be — as long as you don't touch the net trying to block. To avoid net fouls, better blockers keep their hands up while getting ready to block (Fig. 54). This does not provide the left that a good armswing does, but it does eliminate many "nets" called when a blocker comes in contact with the net while using an armswing for a higher jump.

83

(FIG. 55)   *Larry Rundle (No. 11), one of the best blockers in U.S. volleyball,*
blocks one-on-one while playing with Wilt Chamberlain's four-man team, the
Big Dippers, which played top six-man teams on a tour across the country.
Note the position of Rich Riffero, squatting low at the net, ready to play the
ball if it is driven back over the net by the block. (PHOTO: GATHERUM)

56

(FIG. 56)   *Larry Rundle spikes away at a three-man block. Modern volleyball offenses are based on a variety of setting patterns that use all three frontline players as hitters in hopes of freeing one hitter so that he faces no worse than a single, one-on-one block.* (PHOTO: GATHERUM)

Smaller players sometimes use a step or two as an approach to the block for added jump, but this is more likely to result in either a net violation or a mistimed block. Beach doubles players, who cannot afford to reveal the fact they are planning to block, usually stay back a few feet from the net, as if they are playing a normal defense, thus hiding the block until the last possible moment.

Experience will teach you how to ''read'' a hitter so that you will know where he is planning to hit by the way he approaches the ball or turns his body. As you gain that experience, you will be able (if you are a good jumper) to take a position or angle on the block and then, as the hitter prepares to hit toward a different angle, move your arms to that direction, leaving the hitter without a clear shot (Fig. 55–56).

Most balls cleanly blocked at the center of the court will drop back into the opponents' court. Balls blocked at the outer edges of the net will often land out of bounds unless the blocker is facing in the correct direction. Because many strong hitters make an outside approach on a spike (sometimes coming from outside the court to hit a ball set outside near the edge of the court), it is easy for the blocker to get in the habit of facing the hitter at the same angle he is approaching the net. However, a strong block made at this angle will usually send the ball straight back and out of bounds.

To insure that the block will keep the ball inbounds, the blocker should always be facing directly toward the net and not toward the hitter. In addition, the outside blocker

86

should "turn in" or angle his hands to help direct the ball back onto his opponents' court.

A good blocker indoors should be able to reach his forearms above the net, while the average blocker will be able to extend only his wrists above an eight-foot net. As mentioned earlier, the blocker indoors is permitted to reach over the net as long as he does not interfere with the ball before it is hit. On the beach, reaching over the net is not allowed at any time.

Substituting players has become a fine art among coaches of top national and collegiate teams. As a shorter player (a setter or outstanding defensive player) rotates from the back row to the front line, a coach may substitute a taller player who is a good spiker-blocker.

Some coaches will also take advantage of an outstanding blocker on the team by having him switch — after the serve — from one outside blocking position to the center position so he can help double on a block by any of the opposing team's spikers.

Strategy: Beyond the Basics

INDOORS

Volleyball strategy, including offensive and defensive planning, has become quite complicated for indoor teams.

In recent years, leading college, national, and international teams have gone to a variety of two- and three-hitter attacks designed to free a hitter from the two- or three-man block. However, there is sometimes a tendency for teams (and coaches) to spend so much time and effort on developing plays that the necessary practice on the basic skills, such as passing and setting, is sometimes overlooked.

Most teams are probably best off using a simple two-hitter offense. This type of offense is based on having a setter in the front row to receive the pass from his

57

(FIG. 57)   *The setter (No. 9) delivers a high set to a hitter not shown. However, the fake by the center spiker (No. 14) and the threat of a back set help freeze two opposing blockers.* (PHOTO: GATHERUM)

58

(FIG. 58)   *In the three-hitter offense, the setter will come from the back row as the ball is served. Here, the setter (No. 15) is in the center-back position, but lines up just in back of the center front-row player so as to be closer to the net, where he will receive the pass from one of his teammates.*

teammates; then he sets it to one of the two other front-row players for the hit. Although a team must be positioned to receive the serve with three men in the front and three in the back of the court, this offense allows two players to function as the setters — and positioned so that when one is the middle player in the front row, the other is the middle player in the back row. It is thus possible to always have one of them in the front row in any rotation. Because in this offense the other four players are, as they rotate, the hitters, it is sometimes called the four-two offense.

In the two-hitter offense, when the setter in the front row is not in the center position, he switches from either the left or the right outside position to the center of the court as soon as the serve is contacted so that he is ready to receive the pass.

The number of offensive plays is somewhat limited with the two-hitter attack, and the defense can generally key on the other two front-court players as the hitters. (The three backcourt players may spike, but only from at least ten feet back from the net, which greatly limits their hitting threat.)

In the more complicated three-hitter attack, all three front-court players are spikers, with the setter coming from one of the back-row positions.

Again, the two best setters are lined up so that one will always be in the front and the other in the back court. However, because one of the two setters will always be spiking (when he's playing in the front row), this offense requires that the two setters also be good spikers.

91

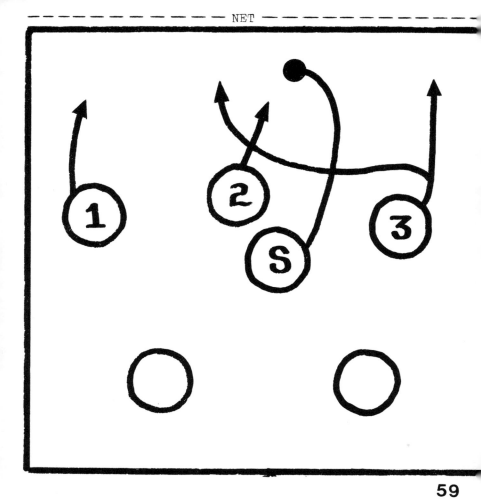

59

(FIG. 59)   *Modern, fast offenses are designed to confuse the defense-particularly the blockers—by increasing the spiking possibilities. In this diagram of a play in the three-hitter attack, the setter (S) comes from the center back-row position to take the pass. He has the options of making the normal set to the outside spiker (1); a short "one set" just above the net to the center hitter (2); a backset to the hitter behind him (3); or, possibly, a low set to the same hitter as he crosses behind the center hitter.*

It was this offense that led Rudy Suwara, volleyball coach at the University of California at Santa Barbara, to convert Gus Mee, the team's Most Valuable Player as a hitter in 1971, into a setter the following year. By the end of the 1972 season, Mee had developed into the team's best setter, and the following year he played as a setter on the U.S. team in the World Games in Moscow.

The three-hitter attack does open up offensive possibilities. For example, a setter coming from the back court to the right center of the court has, among a variety of possible sets, a choice of making: (1) a low, fast "shoot" set or a soft, high set to the left front spiker; (2) a short, quick set just above the net to the center hitter that often leaves the defense no time to block; or (3) a back set to the right front spiker coming behind him (Fig. 57–58).

Some teams also operate a number of offensive patterns in which the front-line spikers cross and switch with one another to confuse the defense (Fig. 59). However, because such plays require not only a good first pass (to allow the setter to come from the back row to receive it) but also precision timing to be effective, the three-hitter offense is never a good choice for the inexperienced or poor-passing team.

Indoor defense is based on taking away the opponents' strongest shot; against the two-hitter attack that most teams operate, that means taking away the spike by the outside hitter.

In this standard defense, the center player in the front row joins in the block against both outside hitters, with the

(FIG. 60)   *The center back-row player (No. 15) has moved in to cover a possible dink, while his teammates guard the channels left to the hitter by the blockers. No. 38 is a front-row player who would be blocking if the spiker were hitting from his side of the court.*

blockers being backed up by the other members of the team.

The two defensive players on the side of the court away from the spiker (in Fig. 60; no. 38, who is in the front row, and no. 40, a back-row player) move in to dig the hard cross court shot. In addition, the front-row player (no. 38) must guard against dinks to his area near the net.

The center player in the back row covers balls hit over the block or off their hands, and usually plays near the back line. (In Fig. 60, he has moved in to cover the dink over the block. This is a good defense when the blockers are tall and jumping high enough to prevent a hitter from spiking over the block.)

The remaining back-row player guards the line behind the block, as well as dinks over the block near the line.

ON THE BEACH

Sand-court defense is not something that can usually be diagramed on a blackboard. It is based instead on learning the hitter's favorite shot, and then trying to take that shot away and force him to hit another spot (or appear to give him his favorite shot and then move there to dig it when he is already committed to hitting it there).

The basic principle of beach defense is: *If the set is back from the net, play defense farther back in the court. If the set is on top of the net, move in closer to the net on defense.*

A beach doubles team can sometimes take advantage of

95

the strengths of one of the partners. For example, when Rudy Suwara, one of the best blockers in the United States, played in a beach tournament with Toshi Toyoda, a defensive standout, they organized a three-play blocking defense they utilized throughout the tournament.

Before serving, Suwara would show Toyoda (and hide from the other team) one, two, or three fingers. One finger meant that he (Suwara) would block the line shot, two fingers that he would block the crosscourt shot, and three fingers that he would just try to block the spiker's best shot, depending on where the set was.

By knowing where his partner would be blocking, Toyoda was free to forget part of the court and concentrate his defense on a specific area.

Some top players, such as Henry Bergmann, studied other players as closely as a Sandy Koufax or Tom Seaver ever studied opposing batters. For example, the word among the best beach players for some time has been that a block was sometimes quite effective against Ron Von Hagen. One of the differences between Bergmann and other top players was that he knew the reason *why* Von Hagen was bothered by a block. (An old wrestling injury prevents Von Hagen from fully extending his arm, limiting his reach on a spike despite an outstanding jump, according to Bergmann).

However, few beach players give any real attention to strategy, according to one of the best of them, Ron Lang. ''Nobody really thinks of how to devise a way to win, other than, say, serve Von Hagen and block.'' Lang says

96

that by "tactically attacking," it's possible to pick up "two or three points a game."

As an example, he tells about playing against Von Hagen and Henry Bergmann in a Santa Barbara tournament. With the match coming up, he told his partner to serve Bergmann — the harder hitter of the two — if it was windy during the game. If it was calm, they would serve Von Hagen. The reasoning behind the move, Lang said, was that Bergmann, who used a bigger armswing for a harder hit, would have more trouble hitting in a wind, where the ball is moving more and is harder to time. It was windy during the match, Lang said, and they served Bergmann and won.

In another windy tournament, this one at San Diego, Lang said he and his teammate made a point always to serve toward the side of the court closest to the beach — the direction from which the wind was coming. Lang said they figured it was more difficult for a player to receive the pass from that direction and then have to set it back into the wind.

Lang also tells about the tournament in which Ernie Suwara was "almost blocking us [Lang and Selznick] out of the tournament" before they decided to try and wear him down. "I told Gene that Ernie [one of the hardest spikers of all time] was to get every serve, every dink. Every time we got in trouble, Ernie was to get the ball. They won the first game, and were leading midway through the second game — his stamina lasted that long — but we went on to win that second game, and the third."

At another tournament, Lang said he violated one of the basic beach strategies (choosing to play into the wind if you win the toss) and instead took the serve, letting the other team have the good side — but, at the same time, letting one of the players know that from the first serve on, he would be receiving every serve in the match. That bit of mental sparring also resulted in a win.

COMMUNICATION

A high ''skyball'' serve is not unlike a high infield fly in baseball, and just as the pitcher usually ''directs traffic'' or tells which player to make the catch, volleyball players generally try to help their teammates by talking to them whenever play calls for it. For example, on the skyball, the player receiving the serve should simply concentrate on watching the ball and be able to rely on his teammate to tell him whether or not the ball will land in or out of bounds.

Communication between players is just as important in beach doubles as it is indoors with six-man teams. The reason why communicating is so important is that with three hits on a side, a volleyball player has to be aware of not only where the ball is at all times, but also where his partner or teammates are, so all three hits can be used to best advantage.

The most common communications are:

On the serve (or any hit during the game), if you see that

the ball will land out of bounds, you should warn a teammate who would play the ball by yelling *"No!"* or *"Out!"* On the skyball, where there is usually plenty of time to gauge where it will land, you should tell him *"It's good!"* as soon as you see that it will land inbounds so that you can move to receive the pass.

The player who is going to receive the serve (especially a skyball or soft hit) should announce it to his teammates by yelling *"Me!"* as soon as he sees he will receive it. (While the skyball is usually used only on the beach, it can be effective indoors. Rudy Suwara tells of the time in the 1969 Five Continents Championship in Montevideo, Uruguay, when the Czechoslovakian team won several games with the aid of a skyball serve. The only team not bothered by it, Suwara says, was East Germany. The Germans simply stood aside on every skyball and let their best player, Arrul Schultz, pass it every time. East Germany beat the Czechs to win the championship.)

Likewise, on a six-man team, after the ball has been passed into the air on the first hit, the player (hopefully, the setter) who is going to make the set should also yell *"Me!"* to avoid confusion and so that the hitters can get into position to spike.

The setter in beach doubles has a couple of calls to make. The indoor spiker expects the block on every play, but the sand-court spiker does not. So, if the setter notices (after the set is in the air) that one of the defensive players is going to block, he should warn his partner by yelling *"He's up!"*

If a set drifts too far back from the net to spike (which often happens outdoors when the wind catches it), the setter should warn his hitter by telling him *"It's back!"* so that he doesn't run underneath the ball. If, on the other hand, the set is right on top of the net, he should tell his partner it is *"Right on!"* or *"Right there!"* so that he knows he can hit it and not have to worry about its drifting over the net.

If the ball is set over the net, the defensive player crosscourt from the play usually has the best view and should yell *"Over!"* as soon as he can so that his partner can make a play on the ball.

If you have to dive to make a play on the ball for the first touch on your side, you should let your partner know (before he sets it) you are able to get up in time to make the third and last hit by shouting *"I'm up!"* If you can't get up to make the last hit, you should tell your partner to *"Go over!"* with the ball on the second hit.

If you are blocking and the ball touches your fingers on the way over the net, you should yell *"One!"* to let your teammate know that they only have two more hits to get the ball over the net.

A defensive dig will often send the ball off wildly, forcing a player to chase it to try and get it back into play. In beach doubles, where the player going after a wild ball has only one partner he can try to get the ball to, he should know where to try to hit the ball from what his partner tells him. If his partner is following right behind him, a call of *"Just up!"* or *"Touch!"* will let him know that if he just

100

gets the ball up into the air, his partner will have a chance to make a play on it.

Until the 1973 beach tournament season, the height of the net on the sand was different from the one indoors. Depending on whether the sand at a local beach was soft or somewhat hard-packed, the net on the beach could be legal at from 7 feet 9 inches to 7 feet 11 inches. But prior to the 1973 season, beach tournament directors voted to standardize the net height at 8 feet, the same as in indoors.

The effect of raising the net two inches from the average 7 feet 10 inches on most beaches (in addition to the four to six inches that most players lose in the sand compared with their indoor jump) was felt mostly by the smaller beach players. Players who could just barely spike with the lower net found themselves hitting more balls into the tape at the top of the net.

Toshi Toyoda, whose 5 feet 7 inches makes him one of the smaller tournament players, noted that the extra two inches also made it harder to dink successfully. That little bit of extra time the ball took to go over and then fall back down two more inches gave some of the bigger but slower defensive players an extra advantage.

Because fewer players could hit straight down with the slightly higher net, most spikes were hit deeper into the court, giving the defense more time to react and make a play, resulting in longer rallies. That made some players, and most spectators, happy about the change.

101

Rules & Referees

RULES & REFEREES

FOLLOWING JUST a few simple rules can turn the wildest "jungle-ball" volleyball game into a good match. The following are the most basic rules.

1. *Play on a net that is eight feet high and taut.* This alone will prevent the wild, free-swinging battle between players standing opposite each other at the middle of a low, droopy net — the most common feature of any jungle-ball game.

2. *Call a violation on anyone touching the net.* This is the proper way to play the game, and strict enforcement of the rule will generally eliminate the roughhouse-type injury caused when players crash into each other at the net.

3. *Try to use all three hits allowed to a team.* Unless the ball is blocked on the way over the net, using all three hits

not only gets more players into the action, but also prevents the game from turning into the one-hit-back-over-the-net that's really not very much fun for the rest of the team.

4. *Use the bump pass.* Every player should learn to use only the bump to receive serves and other balls coming over the net. The player who uses the two-arm bump, instead of hitting the ball back over the net with both hands or with an underhand ''scoop'' shot with the open hands, is already well on the way to learning how to play volleyball the right way.

Although most volleyball rules apply to both the indoor and outdoor versions of the game, there are some differences. These are noted in the following list.

1. Indoors, blockers may reach over the net, but they may not contact the ball until it is hit by the opposing team. (On the beach, reaching over the net is a foul.)

2. Indoors, a hitter may follow through on a hit so that his hand passes over the net. (On the beach, reaching over the net is not allowed at any time.)

3. Indoors, no one is allowed to go under the net or past the centerline while the ball is in play. (On the beach, players are permitted to cross the centerline and go underneath the net onto the opposing team's court in pursuit of a ball that has traveled under the net. However, the player who goes under the net may not interfere with the play of the other team. Interference is a foul.)

103

4. A ball that lands on any part of the line (or rope, outdoors) marking the boundary of the court is good.

5. Indoors, the first team to score 15 points wins. However, a team must win by at least 2 points. (On the beach, most games are played to 11 points. In beach tournaments, undefeated teams play two out of three games to 11 points, while teams that have lost once play each other in single games to 15 points. Beach teams change sides every 4 points. For example, at scores of 3–1, 5–3, 9–3, in 11-point games, and every 5 points in 15-point games, side advantages of wind and sun are evened out.)

6. Double hits (successive contacts) are not allowed except on hard-driven spikes. On spikes, a player may make successive contacts of the ball in a single attempt to play it. For example, a spike driven off a player's arms may carom off his chest without a foul.

7. Indoors, blockers are allowed to make successive contacts of the ball, with the second touch counting as the second of the team's three hits. (On the beach, blockers are not allowed to make successive contacts. The beach player, for example, cannot touch the ball again as it drops off his hand or off the net, while the indoor player can.)

8. Indoors, a line is marked across the court ten feet from the net to denote the "spiking line." Backcourt players must be behind this line when making a spike.

9. Indoors, a ball that crosses the net entirely outside the tape markers on the net (directly above the sideline boundary) is a foul. (On the beach, a ball that crosses the

net outside the net support poles is a foul.)

10. There is no foul on a player who touches the net because it was forced into him by a spike or a driven ball.

11. If two players hold the ball simultaneously above the net, it is a double fault and the serve is played over. However, if the ball is hit simultaneously by two players above the net, the team upon whose side the ball falls is allowed three additional hits to return it. If, on a simultaneous hit, the ball lands on the court, the team on that court is at fault; if it lands outside the court, the team on the other side of the net from where it lands is at fault.

12. A player may go outside of the court to make a play.

13. Indoors, only two time outs, lasting no longer than thirty seconds each, are allowed per game. (On the beach, two one-minute time outs are allowed. Players are also allowed, when play is stopped, to remove sand from their body.)

14. Shouting at an opposing player while he is making a play is a foul.

15. When players on opposing teams commit simultaneous fouls, the serve is played over.

Interpretation of the rules also varies on occasion not only between indoor and beach referees, but also between indoor referees from different countries and even within different areas of the United States.

For example, beach referees are more lenient in their calls on overhand digs than indoor officials. On the beach, the defensive player may take a hard spike with his hands in much the same way he would "set" the ball. That is, the ball may appear to come "visibly to rest" momentarily. This is considered a violation indoors.

However, most of the better beach players play overhand digs the same way as indoor players do, which is to let the ball "slap" off a tightly flexed open palm. If the ball makes a "slap" sound on contact with the hands (just as it would off an arm), it indicates that the ball was not caught or held.

If the ball is not hit hard, or if it's slowed down by striking the net or another player, it must be played cleanly (usually with a bump), even on the beach. An overhand pass or a soft pass or serve will generally result in a violation call by the referee in or out of doors.

Since the 1964 Olympics, indoor referees the world over have allowed sets that previously would have been considered illegal "throws," particularly in the United States.

The general feeling among players and coaches is that the looser interpretation has become necessary in recent years to offset the tremendous advantage the defense had gained, in good part because of taller, higher-jumping players on the block.

In the last few years, most top American referees have followed the guidelines on setting used by the international officials. Many beach players, who adapted to the looser calls on setting while playing indoors, have lately led to a relaxing of the traditionally rigid beach rules concerning the set.

106

(FIG. 61)   *Ed Machado (No. 1) prepares to hit the floor after diving to make a play on a dink shot that has just been dropped over the two blockers at the net.* (PHOTO: GATHERUM)

(FIG. 62)   *Bobby Jackson is shown making a "shoot" at Manhattan Beach. Taking the ball exactly as he would for a jump set, Jackson passed the ball over the head of Kirk Kilgour, left, who was looking for a spike or dink. Used only by a few top beach players, the shoot must be made in* exactly *the direction in which the player making it is facing, and must leave his hands clean, with virtually no spin on the ball, or it will be illegal.* (PHOTO: SCHURMAN)

(FIG. 63) *Most spikers hit their strongest shot at a crosscourt angle. Consequently, most blockers try to take that shot away from the hitter. Here, however, the outside blocker has moved to take away the straight-ahead line shot. Strong hitters will sometimes try to take advantage of this positioning by spiking the ball off the outside blocker's hands so that the ball will go out of bounds off the block. In this case, the hitter decided to dink over the block.* (PHOTO: VAN WAGNER)

(FIG. 64) *Henry Berg mann watches as one of hi spikes blasts past Ron Lang* (PHOTO: GATHERUM)

65

(FIG. 65–66) *Two views of the man who never lets up on the volleyball court, Ron Von Hagen. In Fig.* 65 *Von Hagen strains to make a one-arm bump of a well-placed dink.* (PHOTO: SCHURMAN). *In Fig.* 66, *Von Hagen charges off the court, scattering the crowd, to make a bump back over his head in order to keep the ball in play.* (PHOTO: GATHERUM)

66

Ron Lang, one of the premier setters among beach players, said recently that it is getting more difficult to determine just what a throw is on the beach. "When I first started playing [1956], you had to set the way you were facing or it was a throw. Now, more and more beach referees are allowing a player to face one way and then make a lateral set, off to one side."

The change, Lang said, makes it "harder to ref." Where, he said, do you "draw the line . . . do you let the player turn the set [make a lateral set, and not in the direction he's facing] just a little? Or do you allow him to turn it a lot?" As Lang noted, there's little room for argument when the setter must set directly in front (or, in the case of a backset, directly in back) of the way he is facing. Although beach refereeing on the set remains much more strict than indoors, several players are complaining that the rules have become too loose and are hurting the beach game.

In addition to the direction of the set, the actual touch or handling of the set has been influenced by the international game.

For years, beach players with good hands and the soft touch had been the standard by which setting in the United States was judged. However, after 1964, most of the U.S. players realized that in international competition referees were again allowing sets that Americans were used to seeing called throws.

In international matches, players were allowed to "hold" a set — in the eyes of the U.S. teams — as well as turn it laterally.

Rudy Suwara, volleyball coach at UCSB and both a U.S. Olympic player and an AAA beach player, said that refereeing indoors has pretty much "stabilized," allowing a more relaxed interpretation of the rules. However, he said, "the East Coast is still ten years behind . . . they still don't allow setters to hold and direct the set as we do on the West Coast."

Suwara is in favor of the change in refereeing, particularly on the touch. "I think it's penalty enough if the set is slightly mishandled because there is a loss of control," he said. "Some refs want everybody to have perfect hands, but there just aren't that many setters with hands like Toshi [Toyoda] and Jack Henn."

The other main influence of international volleyball has been on the dink. As with the indoor set, players are now being allowed almost to catch or hold the soft hit with the fingertips, and direct it much the same way a basketball player will direct a one-armed pass. On the beach, however, a player must still not allow the ball to stop or come to rest in his hand on the dink, but instead must hit it cleanly.

Most volleyball games are played without a referee. In beach volleyball, the calls for infractions are usually left up to the honor of the player making the violation.

Even in tournaments, where there are referees, many beach players will make calls against themselves if the referee missed it. Of course, there are some players who would never make *any* call that the referee missed, but in volleyball they seem to be the exception rather than the rule.

111

In more than one beach tournament, a player has called a "net" violation on himself in the closing stages on the finals and lost the match because of it.

Other players will call the obvious fouls — the "net" or "throw" that is obvious to all — but at the same time will ignore the times they just barely brush the net while making a good spike. The problem, of course, is where does such a player draw the line between making a call against himself and ignoring it? The easiest and best way is simply to call every violation.

HOW TO REFEREE

Every referee is going to miss a call sooner or later. But, as Henry Bergmann has noted, the worst mistake a referee can make is to try to even out the calls — that is, if you miss one for one team, ignore one made by the other team to square it. Trying to make up for one mistake by making another is the fastest way for a referee to lose control of the game.

Another good rule is never to let a bad team cheat a good one. What that means is, if both teams are playing at a low-skilled level, a referee might allow some leniency in his calls. But the ref should never allow a bad team to take advantage of a better team by giving it the benefit of the doubt on judgment calls. For example, it would not be right to allow one team to get away with continual setting violations that the better team is just not making.

The biggest problem for many inexperienced referees is concentrating on watching for infractions and not getting so involved in watching a good rally that they forget about the job they are supposed to be doing.

The best seat for a referee (indoors or out) is above the net on the ref's platform at the end of the net. From here the referee has a clear view of the action above the net. This is particularly important on the beach, where reaching over the net is not allowed.

Some beach referees prefer to sit on the sand, just outside the rope boundaries, underneath the net. However, on most plays, the net blocks the view from this position on any play above the net.

Referees in a beach tournament, which may have up to twelve games going at the same time, are usually the players themselves. A member of the winning team will remain on the court and officiate the next match.

THE COURT AND EQUIPMENT

The ball: For both indoor and sand-court play, better players use leather volleyballs. They cost more than the rubber ones used by most schools and playgrounds, but they are well worth the difference in price.

Better quality leather balls have twelve- or eighteen-panel covers. The official ball for United States Volleyball Association Championship play is the twelve-panel (or twelve-patch) S V-5 Star, made by H.E. Wilson and Company, Encino, California. Recently many col-

113

(FIG. 67)   *Larry "Rags" Rundle, maybe the best all-around volley-ball player in the U.S., warms up prior to a match at Manhattan.*
(PHOTO: VAN WAGNER)

(FIG. 68)   *Ron Lang, wh teamed first with Gene Se nick and later with Ron V Hagen to dominate bea volleyball for nearly t years, from 1958 to 196* (PHOTO: SCHURMAN)

(FIG. 69)   *Bobby Garcia, at 5'9" one of the smallest AAA-rated beach players, drives a spike past the block of 7'1" Wilt Chamberlain at the Manhattan Open.* (PHOTO: SCHURMAN)

(FIG. 70)   *Chamberlain, one foot still in the sand, reaches high above the eight-foot net in an unsuccessful attempt to block a shot by Miles Pabst, outstanding player of the year, during the 1973 indoor volleyball season.* (PHOTO: SCHURMAN)

(FIG. 71) *Larry Rundle, center, playing up close to the net, puts his hands up to make an overhand dig of a hard spike. If the hand is open and rigid, the ball will come off the defensive player with a clean slap sound. If the ball is caught or held even momentarily on an overhand dig, many referees will call a foul.* (PHOTO: VAN WAGNER)

(FIG. 72) *Ron Von Hagen fakes a hit on an overset during the finals of the 1973 Santa Barbara Open.* (PHOTO: VAN WAGNER)

(FIG. 73) *A tape shot is a hit, like the one made here by John Vallely, that strikes the two-inch taped portion of the top of the net. Even a hard spike will sometimes just drop over the net after being slowed down by the tape. As a result, better defensive players instinctively move closer to the net as soon as they see a ball hit the tape.* (PHOTO: SCHURMAN)

(FIG. 74) *Keith Erickson (No. 7), a professional basketball star with the Los Angeles Lakers and Phoenix Suns, was one of the best spikers in the U.S. during his volleyball career, which took him from beach tournaments to the Olympics.* (PHOTO: VAN WAGNER)

lege teams switched to another ball by the same company, the eighteen-patch SV-W.

Sand-court and beach players prefer a somewhat heavier ball outdoors, one that is less affected by wind. The ball most often found on California beaches is the eighteen-patch laceless leather ball made by Spaulding. Beach players sometimes use twelve-patch balls, but the eighteen-patch models tend to be slightly heavier and also seem to hold their roundness better over a longer period of time.

The way to tell the difference between an indoor and an outdoor ball is to look at the seams where the panels or patches come together. An outdoor ball is sewn together with the stitching just barely visible, tucked under where the panels are joined. Indoor balls do not have sewn seams.

When you buy a ball, the most important quality to look for is roundness. Toss the ball spinning into the air. If it is lopsided or out of balance, it should be apparent in the spin. You should also check the seams to make sure there are no irregularities.

The best conditioning for a volleyball is simply to play with it. A new ball is sometimes stiff, but as it gets older it develops a better "feel." As they become worn, beach volleyballs also tend to get somewhat heavier as they absorb the combination of hand oils and sweat during play. As a result, the balls used in beach tournaments are usually at least a few months old.

A few tournament officials, faced with the prospect of

it with sand. Generally speaking, the best sand for a court is the finest (least coarse) kind available.

It is preferable to situate the outdoor court so that the prevailing wind blows directly parallel with the net. With the court set up this way, the wind will have a minimum effect on play.

Rope is the best line marker for a sand court because it jumps when struck by a ball, making it easy for players to spot whether a ball landed on the line (which is considered "in") or just outside.

It is easy to make up a set of rope markers out of quarter-inch rope. At each corner of the court, attach a length of rope about three feet long with a scrap of wood at one end. Bury the wood into the sand to insure that the ropes will not be pulled out of line during play.

121

Physical Conditioning

Jumping ability is as important in volleyball as it is in basketball, and in both sports tall players have an advantage.

Although volleyball is attracting more and more tall players — many of them former basketball stars — several of the top players in the game are no more than six feet or, in some instances, several inches less.

The smaller volleyball player, however, must have a jump that makes up for his lack of height. How much of a jump?

To be able to spike a volleyball down at a sharp angle, you should be able at least to touch a regulation ten-foot-high basketball rim. In fact, all of the best spikers in both beach and indoor volleyball can jump even higher — most of them can slam dunk a basketball.

Wilt Chamberlain, who can slam dunk with the best of them, can also very nearly spike a volleyball straight down. But Chamberlain, at seven feet, with long arms as well, can stand flat-footed and reach as high as most average-sized men can reach jumping.

At the other extreme, there is Toshi Toyoda. A good example of the "little man" in volleyball, Toyoda has played for Japan's national team, was later an All American at UCLA, and has been a top-rated AAA beach player. While he is known primarily for setting and defensive skills, Toyoda is also an effective spiker and blocker because of his jumping ability.

Where the average man jumps maybe eighteen to twenty-two inches from a standing position, Toyoda has jumped *40 inches*. To give an idea of just how good a jump that is, it should be noted that Valery Bugalayenkov, the outstanding spiker on the Russian Olympic team in 1964 and 1968, once had a standing jump of forty-two inches—beating a close friend in a spur-of-the-moment competition by one-half inch. The friend with the 41½-inch jump was Valery Brumel, who held the world high-jump mark at 7 feet 5¾ inches from 1963 to 1971.

While good jumping ability is absolutely necessary for the smaller player, the increasing number of bigger players going into volleyball (as in every sport) is forcing players even well over six feet to realize that they can no longer get by on just their natural spring.

For those looking for a way to increase their jump, the answer is exercise — and, in most cases, weight lifting.

123

75

(FIG. 75)   *Sand flying, Larry Rundle powers a spike between the brothers Lee, Greg and Jon, during a tournament at Santa Barbara's East Beach.* (PHOTO: GATHERUM)

The Cuban team that beat the U.S. team in Olympic qualifications in 1972 is probably the best recent example of what weight training can do for volleyball players. Rudy Suwara, who was the captain of the U.S. team, said that several of the Cubans had a Sargent (or standing) jump of over forty inches, while the best of them could do forty-four inches. With a running start, some of the Cubans jumped over forty-eight inches, while two or three could jump an incredible fifty inches.

All of the Cuban players were on a heavy weight-exercise program, he said, and one of them was reportedly doing leg presses with an almost unheard of 1,100 pounds.

Probably the first thing to do before starting an exercise program is to have a physical checkup. The second thing is to determine just what your jump actually is.

One way is to stand next to a wall and mark the highest point of your reach against the wall. Then chalk your fingertips, bend down, and, without taking a step, leap as high as possible, touching the wall with your chalked fingers at the top of your jump. (This is one version of the Sargent jump. There are Sargent boards available. They can be adjusted to the reach of any individual and will show at a glance the jump in inches as the jumper places his fingertips against the board.)

It's a good idea to keep a chart of how your jump progresses throughout the six months to a year that make up a well-planned weight-training and exercise program.

Several volleyball players have claimed increases of from seven to nine inches in their Sargent jumps in a single year of intensive weight training. That additional seven to nine inches — combined with practice and experience — can be the difference in becoming a good spiker rather than just an average hitter.

WEIGHT EXERCISES

Most volleyball coaches and players seem to be convinced that the best exercise program combines weight training and nonweight exercises.

Although most of the emphasis on weight lifting for volleyball is naturally on the legs, it's important to remember that increased strength in the wrists and arms will enable you to spike a ball that much harder.

The *squat* is the basic weight exercise for volleyball. Some coaches in various sports, particularly football, have warned against doing "full squats" on the theory that there is an increased likelihood of a knee injury.

However, most volleyball exercise programs, including those designed for recent U.S. national teams, have included the full squat (where you squat until the backs of your thighs touch a low bench).

A good program of squat exercises includes the following:

1. Warm up with three sets of ten repetitions of full squats with a lightweight barbell (about one-third of your body weight).

126

2. Using a barbell with half your body weight, do five sets of ten repetitions of full squats. Eventually, work up to one set of fifty with two-thirds of your body weight.

3. For maximum leg strength, do half squats in four sets of five repetitions. The average-sized man (150–165 pounds) should start with a weight of about 140–150 pounds and do one set of ten repetitions for the first day. If not stiff the following day, increase the weight from ten to thirty pounds; repeat the one set of ten repetitions for the next three workout days before moving on to the four-sets-of-five program.

4. After doing no. 3, increase the weight slightly and do five sets of four repetitions of half squats.

In all weight exercises, it is best not only to work under a knowledgeable weight coach, but also to start with *light* rather than heavy weights in each exercise. Increasing the weight as you become more accustomed to it is the best way to lessen the chance of injury.

In addition to squats, other exercises, including leg presses on a weight machine and bench presses for the upper body, are also useful.

There is sometimes a tendency to overdo weight lifting, letting it become a daily routine. Most weight lifters feel that it is best to do weight work every other day, or three days a week, in order to let muscle cells rebuild after a heavy workout.

JUMPING EXERCISES

There are several other exercises that volleyball players have found will increase jumping ability — even without weight training.

One, which was developed by the Russians, is the *depth jump*. In this exercise, you simply step off a table (about three feet high) and, as both feet hit the ground, you explode quickly into as high a jump as possible. Do two sets of ten repetitions. High jumpers such as Russia's Brumel and Pat Matzdorf of the United States, also a former world record holder, credit a good part of their jumping success to this exercise.

Another exercise, which can be done with or without weights, is the *jump squat*. The jump squat, as the term implies, involves squatting to a nearly full-squat position and then jumping as high as possible, again and again. Beach players, who do this exercise in soft sand, sometimes hold dumbbells weighing fifteen to twenty-five or more pounds in each hand. Some volleyball players have increased their jump substantially just by doing this exercise about a hundred times or repetitions a day.

If you are not doing jump squats in soft sand, it is a good idea to use about two thicknesses of tumbling mats to ease the shock on your knees.

Another common leg-building exercise among serious volleyball players is the *running of stadium steps*. Running up the steps of a local high school or college football stadium — taking two or three steps at a time — has for some time been considered a top conditioning exercise for track and football players. Volleyball players have found that it helps their jump, as well as their stamina.

If you are doing weight-lifting exercises, you can run the steps on your "days off" from the weights. It is also beneficial not only to sprint up the steps but also to jog, rather than walk, on the way down. Running the steps about five times in succession is about as much as most good athletes do.

However, one way to increase the effort is to wear a ten- to twenty-pound weight belt such as the one skin divers use. (The weight belt can also be used in the jump squats in place of dumbbells held in the hands.)

In addition to other exercises, most of the better beach volleyball players run on the beach. But when they run, they do not run on the hard-packed sand near the water, but instead on the soft sand. The soft sand makes the running more difficult, and it acts as a reminder that there is a difference between moving through the soft sand on a beach volleyball court and running on the hardwood floor of an indoor one.

Many top volleyball players have arrived at a beach tournament in good physical condition from exercising and playing indoors, only to find themselves stumbling through the unfamiliar, soft sand.

WARM-UP EXERCISES

Warming-up exercises are sometimes taken for

129

granted, but the results can be a painful and serious injury.

Although most top beach players are in peak condition during the summer tournament season, nearly all of them have some sort of warm-up routine they do before playing a game, either in a tournament or in a friendly pick-up match during the week.

A common routine includes:

Toe-touchers: Stand with feet shoulder-width apart, touch toes, and without bending your knees, touch either knuckles or palms to the ground between your feet, and then again, as far back between your legs as you can reach. Repeat ten times.

Hurdler's stretch: Sit on the ground with one leg stretched out in front of you and the other back — like a runner clearing a hurdle — and touch your head to your knee without bending your outstretched leg. Repeat ten times, then switch leg positions and do again.

Bump and set the ball back and forth, and then make a few practice serves to become familiar with the ball (and, outdoors, with the wind).

Hit the volleyball into the net, not too hard at the beginning, increasing the power until your arm and shoulder are loose and you are spiking the ball into the net. (If someone holds the rope at the bottom of the taut net during this exercise, the ball will bounce off the net right back to the hitter.)

Practice a few spikes, first tossing the ball to your partner, who sets it for the hit.

The most important warm up, both physically and

130

mentally, takes place before the start of the first game of the day. After the first competition, you are usually loose enough to keep playing the rest of the day with only a minimum of warm up before subsequent games. However, many players find it difficult to get fired up mentally for the first game. One way, used by a few top players, is to go through a very quick, hard game of "pepper" — spiking the ball back and forth at each other at close range. Some pro football players, following the same line of thinking, have a linebacker give them a whack in the helmet just before the start of a game, feeling that, after that, the first contact in the game won't come as much of a shock. In those first, sometimes crucial points of a game, the players who are most ready have a big advantage.

FOOD, DRINK, AND DIET

Diet is as important in volleyball as it is in other sports. Although some athletes are more diet-conscious than others, most of the top AAA beach players are careful about what they eat and drink before facing an exhausting two-day midsummer beach tournament.

Of course, not all of them agree on just what is good diet practice. But through experimentation over years of playing all day long in the hot sand, most have developed a personal diet that seems to get them through a tournament.

Because the last matches of a beach tournament, particularly the finals, are often decided when cramps hit

131

one of the players, the players capable of making it to the finals of an open tournament are the ones most concerned with diet.

Henry Bergmann, for example, had trouble early in his volleyball career with cramps during tournaments, and so he began reading books on diet and nutrition to see if he could come up with an answer to the problem.

He found that part of the solution was simply getting into better condition. A dominating hitter, Bergmann said that he generally did not get the serve (so that he would not be the hitter in a doubles game) at his home beach. Playing in a tournament with a good partner, he found he was being served all the time — forcing him to do most of the running, jumping, and hitting for his team.

He also said an increase in calcium in his diet, plus drinking plenty of fluids during a tournament, also helped ease his tendency to cramp.

Marathon runners in particular have found that endurance and performance increase as the amount of fluids taken before and during an event is increased. If you wait until you are thirsty before taking your first drink during a tournament or marathon, you've already lost enough body fluid to affect how you will perform.

Actually, quite a bit has been written on athletic diets, particularly in the area of track and field, where performances are easily measured. Some of the basic theories that appear often in works on nutrition and diet for the athlete are as follows:

1. Eating carbohydrates for increased and sustained energy. Athletes in several sports have found that a high-protein diet (meat, fish, eggs, dairy products, and nuts) begun about a week before an athletic event, followed by a high-carbohydrate diet (bread, potatoes, cereal grains, and spaghetti) for two or three days before the event, is the best diet yet developed for endurance.

2. Lowering salt intake. Some nutritionists feel there is enough salt in the average American diet to make additional salt (from a shaker) unnecessary. Several top volleyball players have said that, after eliminating table salt from their diet, they perform better and sweat less in the hot beach weather. (Most of them also suggest that the best time to cut back on salt intake is during the cooler winter months, so that the body can adjust to the change by the time summer arrives.) At the same time, most beach players avoid taking salt tablets during even the hottest tournaments on the theory that it is more important to drink enough liquids. Salt tablets sometimes cause problems, especially if they are taken without enough fluids. Those who do take salt tablets should be sure to take only the "buffered" variety (they are easier on the stomach), with a pint of water for each half tablet.

3. Many of the better tournament players, like many other athletes, have found that drinking Gatorade seems to be the best way to replace what the body loses in sweat during physical exertion. Others prefer drinking liquids such as herb tea, strained orange juice, or plain water.

Although it would seem to be only common sense,

133

many people, players as well as spectators, go all day to a beach volleyball game and think nothing about the sun until they are already home and *sunburned*. Hats, sunglasses, and sun-tan lotions are the most basic items anyone should take along to a tournament or even just a day at the beach.

Some Final
Notes

There were fifty-two sanctioned beach tournaments scheduled in California last year, including events for women, four- and six-man teams, and mixed (coed) teams.

Most of the tournaments were either B, A, AA, or open beach doubles tournaments for men. Under the ratings system used by the Santa Monica Recreation and Parks Department, the organization that oversees beach competition, anyone who has never played or placed in a beach volleyball tournament has a B classification. B tournaments are usually a bit ragged, with some inexperienced players, but the top finishers are generally solid players, some of them with a strong indoor volleyball background.

A player moves up in classification by winning or finishing high in a tournament. For example, a player can

135

achieve an A rating by winning a B tournament, by finishing second through seventh in an AA tournament, or by finishing eighth or ninth in an open tournament.

While a player may play in a tournament held for his classification or a higher rating, he may not play in a tournament for a lower rating. For example, an A player may plan in an A, AA, or open tournament, but not in a B event.

Thus, the opens are open to any player. In practice, the players in an open almost all have AA or AAA ratings — the highest in beach volleyball. And of the fifty-six players who started the 1973 season with AAA ratings, only ten won an open that year.

During the 1973 summer season, an informal poll to rank the top beach players was taken among the players themselves. As expected, there were differences of opinion as to who was the best setter, the best spiker, the best all-around player, and so on. But in one category — desire to win — the vote was almost unanimous for Ron Von Hagen.

Four individual players were rated time and again as the best in any given beach tournament. They were Von Hagen, Matt Gage, Larry Rundle, and Henry Bergmann. The other players mentioned most often, listed generally in the order of votes they received, were: John Vallely, Buzz Swartz, Bob Clem, Tom Chamales, Bobby Jackson, Greg Lee, Bill Imwalle, Ron Lang, Kirk Kilgour, and Fred Zuelich.

136

On individual skills, the players named were: *serve* — Lang; *passing* — Rundle; *setting* — Lang and Von Hagen; *hitting* — Bergmann and Gage; *blocking* — Rundle and Gage; *defense* — Lang, Swartz, and Chamales.

Modern volleyball offenses and defenses have become increasingly complex, so much so that they are of interest mostly to the top national and collegiate teams. Teams with less experience usually benefit by learning a simple game plan and then concentrating on making their game mistake-free. However, for those interested in the more advanced game, a good source of information is *Winning Volleyball* by Allen E. Scates (Boston: Allyn & Bacon). Scates, head volleyball coach at UCLA and coach of the U.S. Olympic and Pan American teams, is one of the game's top strategists, and he discusses indoor strategy in great detail in this book.

If a picture is worth a thousand words, an hour or two with a good volleyball player is worth at least two or three pictures. Volleyball clinics have been springing up all over southern California in the last few years, some taught by top beach and indoor players. Rudy Suwara, a former Olympian, an AAA beach player, and volleyball coach at the University of California, Santa Barbara, has offered a well-received one-day clinic for audiences ranging from high school gym classes to experienced players and

137

coaches. He may be contacted in care of the Physical Activities Office at the UCSB.

WHERE TO GO

Most southern California beaches have at least a few volleyball nets, and on any given day it's possible to see top players in action at almost any one of them.

The most popular volleyball beaches are the ones on which the summer tournaments are played, and it is here that a visitor looking for good beach volleyball will find it.

From north to south, these beaches include: East Beach, in Santa Barbara; Will Rogers State Beach, Sorrento Beach, and the Santa Monica Pier, in Santa Monica; Playa del Rey; Rosecrans Street, Marine Avenue, and the Manhatten Pier, in Manhattan Beach; the Hermosa Pier, in Hermosa Beach; Corona del Mar State Beach; Main Beach, in Laguna; and Ocean Beach, in San Diego.

Further information about the tournaments may be obtained from the Santa Monica Recreation and Parks Department, Santa Monica, California.

Glossary

Ace A serve that either lands untouched, for a point, or is to difficult to return.

BALL ON A call made on the beach when a ball from another court rolls onto your court during play. The call may be made by the players or a referee. Play stops immediately and the ball is served again by the same team.

BLOCK A defensive play in which a player jumps, reaching above the net to stop an offensive hit at the net.

BUMP A pass from one player to another using the inside of the wrists and forearms.

CUTSHOT An offensive hit in which a player, instead of hitting with power, slices the ball just over and parallel to the net.

139

Dig   A defensive play aimed at bringing a spiked ball up into play.

Dink   A soft shot hit just over the net or over a blocker's hands.

Double hit   When a ball hits a player twice in succession. A double hit is legal on a hard-driven spike but is a foul on a serve, on a spike that slows down by hitting the net on the way over, or on a shot that is not hit hard.

Double foul   When players on both teams commit simultaneous fouls, the play is taken over (the serving team serves again).

Draw   The place in the bracketings or pairings of teams in a tournament that determines which teams a team will be playing against. An "easy draw" means that in the early rounds of a tournament a team will be playing against weaker opponents.

Fake   When a hitter, to keep the defense back, fakes a spike swing at a ball that he realizes is over the net.

Floater   A serve delivered without spin, so that it acts like a knuckleball pitch in baseball.

Foot foul   When a player steps on or over the back line while serving.

Free ball   When a team is forced into trouble by a bad pass or set and must bump pass the ball over the net just to keep the ball in play, but in doing so gives the other team an easy ball to play.

Net   A foul called when any player touches the net during play. The call should be made by the player committing the infraction.

OVER A foul called in beach play when a player reaches over the net when hitting, faking a hit, or blocking. While beach players are prohibited from reaching over the net, indoor players may reach over to block (but they may not contact the ball before it is hit).

OVERSET A set that comes over the net onto the side of the defensive team.

QUICK SERVE A serve made before the opposing team is ready. The other team must be ready and facing the server before a serve can be made.

ROUNDHOUSE An overhand serve with top spin, which causes the ball to drop.

SAND A call made by a player after play is stopped to delay the next serve until sand can be removed from his body.

SCREENING When a player blocks the view of the server from players of the opposing team. All players on the opposing team must have a clear view of the server before the serve can be made.

SHOOT A two-handed set that is used as a shot over the net, usually as a dink.

SIDEOUT When the serving team fails to score during a play and the ball goes over to the other team.

SKYBALL A very high, underhand serve used on the beach.

SPIKE A hard, downward hit.

TAPE SHOT When a ball is hit or spiked into the tape at the top of the net and continues on over the net.

THROW A foul occurring when the ball is mishandled and not set or hit cleanly.

Dewey Schurman

The author was born on May 29, 1943, and raised in Los Angeles. He spent a good part of his life on the beaches of southern California. A graduate of the University of California, Santa Barbara (1966), for the last three years he has been a staff writer for the Santa Barbara *News-Press*. The author is married and has two children.

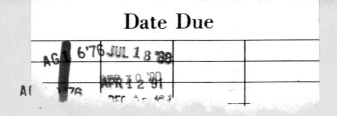